Food With Succulent Flavors

AMBIKA PATHANIA

BlueRose Publishers

First Published in November 2020

ISBN: 978-93-5427-067-3

Price: INR 179/-

BLUEROSE PUBLISHERS

www.bluerosepublishers.com

info@bluerosepublishers.com

+91 8882 898 898

Cover Design:

Sanya Rastogi

Typographic Design:

Tanya Raj Upadhyay

Distributed by: BlueRose, Amazon, Flipkart, Shopclues

DEDICATED

To the Ones who are Reading this.
Thank You!

QUOTE

One Day! I'm Gonna Make The Onions Cry ☺

ACKNOWLEDGEMENTS

Let's just quickly do this, for all the help I've received from some of the quirky people in my life to come up with this book.

Gokul, my foremost reader for giving the script some thoughtful amendments and suggestions as it's and bits!

My sister Ishita, for keeping hopes and patience high for this exciting piece to get released.

Father, mother, sisters, brothers, extended family, & friends -- you all know your contributions, therefore, feel free to extort the credit as much you like. Kisses & Hugs!

CONTENTS

DELIGHTFUL SMOOTHIES

FRESH AND FRUITY ALWAYS

MANGO SPINACH SMOOTHIE

TYPE: Gluten-free; Nut-free; Soy-free, and, Refined sugar-free

YIELD: 2-3 servings

TIME-TAKEN: 5-10 minutes

INGREDIENTS ON THE GO

- 2 cups frozen diced mango
- 2 cups spinach
- 1 cup yogurt
- 1/2 cup milk
- 2 tbsp flaxseeds

DIRECTIONS TO BE FOLLOWED

- All you need to do is combine all the above-mentioned ingredients in a blender until smooth.
- Pour into bowls and top with toppings (like mango, kiwi, blueberries, OR coconut flakes).
- Serve it with a bit of flaxseed or cinnamon on it.

PINKLICIOUS SMOOTHIE

TYPE: Gluten-free; Nut-free; Soy-free, and, Refined sugar-free

YIELD: 2-3 servings

TIME-TAKEN: 5-10 minutes

INGREDIENTS ON THE GO

- 1.5 cups coconut milk
- 1 cup strawberries
- 1 cup raspberries
- 1 peeled orange
- 1 coarsely chopped carrot
- 1 peeled beetroot
- 1/2 cup chopped zucchini
- 1/2 cup roasted cashews

DIRECTIONS TO BE FOLLOWED

- All you need to do is add all above-mentioned ingredients to a blender and blend until smooth.
- Serve and Enjoy!

IMMUNE BOOSTER SMOOTHIE

TYPE: Gluten-free; Refined sugar-free, and Soy-free

YIELD: 2-3 servings

TIME-TAKEN: 5-10 minutes

INGREDIENTS ON THE GO

- 2 bananas
- 1 peeled orange
- 1 cup milk
- 1 spinach
- 1/2 cup raspberries
- 1/4 peeled beetroot
- 1/4 cup yogurt
- 1 inch chunked ginger
- 1 tbsp peanut butter

DIRECTIONS TO BE FOLLOWED

- All you need to do is mix all the above-mentioned ingredients in a blender until smooth.
- Pour into bowls and top with toppings (like fresh berries, granola, or coconut flakes).
- Serve and Enjoy!

MOCHA SMOOTHIE

TYPE: Gluten-free; Refined sugar-free, and Soy-free

YIELD: 2-3 servings

TIME-TAKEN: 5-10 minutes

INGREDIENTS ON THE GO

- 1.5 bananas
- 1 cup oat milk
- 1/2 cup chopped zucchini
- 1/4 cup roasted cashews
- 3 dates
- 1 tbsp cocoa powder
- 1 shot espresso/instant coffee
- 1/2 tbsp vanilla extract

DIRECTIONS TO BE FOLLOWED

- All you need to do is mix all the above-mentioned ingredients in a blender until smooth.
- Pour into bowls and top with toppings (like berries, coconut flakes, or chocolate chips)
- Serve and Enjoy every sip!

ORANGE GINGER SMOOTHIE

TYPE: Gluten-free; Refined sugar-free, and, Soy-free

YIELD: 2-3 servings

TIME-TAKEN: 5-10 minutes

INGREDIENTS ON THE GO

- 2 small oranges OR 1 medium orange
- 1 peeled ginger
- 1 carrot
- 3/4 cup mangoes
- 1/2 cup raspberries
- 3/4 cup milk
- 1/2 cup yogurt
- 2 tbsp hemp seeds

DIRECTIONS TO BE FOLLOWED

- All you need to do is mix all the above-mentioned ingredients in a blender until smooth.
- Pour into bowls and top with toppings (like banana, pineapple chunks, or coconut milk)
- Serve and Enjoy every sip!

BLUEBERRY BANANA SMOOTHIE

TYPE: Gluten-free; Nut-free; and, Soy-free

YIELD: 2-3 servings

TIME-TAKEN: 5-10 minutes

INGREDIENTS ON THE GO

- 1 cup blueberries
- 1 frozen banana (preferably ripped)
- 1 cup of water
- 1 cup yogurt
- Honey
- Chia seeds

DIRECTIONS TO BE FOLLOWED

- Put all the ingredients in a blender in the order of appearance
- Blend the ingredients in a high-speed blender for 2-3 minutes until you get a smooth and creamy texture.
- Taste the smoothie, adding more water if it is too thick or adding a sweetener of choice if it's not sweet enough for you.
- Add the fresh fruit toppings like (Sliced Banana and blueberries) for garnish.
- Enjoy cold immediately, or store in the refrigerator for up to 24 hours.

DARK CHOCOLATE PEANUT BUTTER BANANA SMOOTHIE

TYPE: Gluten-free; and, Soy-free

YIELD: 2-3 servings

TIME-TAKEN: 5-10 minutes

INGREDIENTS ON THE GO

- 2 cups water (360 mL), or yogurt or any plant-based milk
- 1 cup peanut butter
- 1 tablespoon dark chocolate or unsweetened cocoa powder
- 2 bananas frozen

DIRECTIONS TO BE FOLLOWED

- Put all ingredients into a blender and mix until smooth.
- Pour into the bowl along with the toppings (like sliced bananas and Chocolate chips)

GREEN SMOOTHIE

TYPE: Gluten-free; Nut-free; and, Soy-free

YIELD: 2-3 servings

TIME-TAKEN: 10 minutes

INGREDIENTS ON THE GO

- 2 cups leafy greens(spinach)
- 2 cups water or coconut water or any plant based milk
- 1 banana frozen
- 1 cup peach
- 1 cup pineapple
- 1 cup mixed berries

DIRECTIONS TO BE FOLLOWED

- Blend leafy greens and water first.
- Add fruits and blend again.
- Enjoy!

Special Tip: Use at least one frozen fruit to chill smoothie.

ALMOND AND DATES SMOOTHIE

TYPE: Gluten-free; and, Soy-free

YIELD: 2-3 servings

TIME-TAKEN: 5-10 minutes

INGREDIENTS ON THE GO

- 1 ½ cups unsweetened almond milk
- 1 cup dates
- 1 banana frozen
- 2 tablespoons almond butter
- 1 tablespoon honey (optional)
- 1 cup of ice cubes

DIRECTIONS TO BE FOLLOWED

- In a bowl combine the almond milk and dates; cover and chill overnight. (Or place dates in a heatproof bowl and cover with boiling water; let it stand for 10 minutes. Drain and cool slightly.) Enjoy cold immediately, or store in the refrigerator for up to 24 hours.
- In a blender combine milk, dates, banana, almond butter, and if desired, honey. Cover and blend 30 seconds or until smooth.
- Add ice and blend until smooth.
- Enjoy every sip!

MANGO CHIA SEEDS SMOOTHIE

TYPE: Gluten free; and, Soy free

YIELD: 2-3 servings

TIME-TAKEN: 5-10 minutes

INGREDIENTS ON THE GO

- 2 tablespoons chia seeds
- 1 ½ cups unsweetened almond milk
- 2 medium bananas - sliced
- 2 cups frozen mango chunks

DIRECTIONS TO BE FOLLOWED

- Put all ingredients into a blender and mix until smooth.
- Pour into a bowl along with the toppings (like slices of mangoes).
- Enjoy!

DAY onto BREAKFAST

ENJOY YOUR MORNING WITH US

OATMEAL PANCAKES

TYPE: Soy-free; Nut-free; and, Gluten-free

YIELD: 8/10 Pancakes

TIME-TAKEN: 20-25 Minutes

INGREDIENTS ON THE GO

- 2 cups oats
- 1 cup milk
- 1/3rd cup apple sauce
- 2 Tbsp maple syrup
- 1 Tbsp melted coconut oil
- 1 Tbsp baking powder
- 2 Tbsp ground cinnamon
- 1 Tbsp vanilla extract
- 1/2 Tbsp salt

DIRECTIONS TO BE FOLLOWED

- Blend the oatmeal until turned into a flour.
- Mix all the ingredients in a bowl.
- Pre-heat frying pan (add a bit of oil, if your pan is non-stick); add 1/4th cup batter onto the pan and keep cooking. Flip the pancakes when they are bubbly and sides are firm enough nearly abt 2-3 minutes and vice-versa.
- Do the topping (like maple syrup, almonds, pistachios, or any sweet syrup).
- Enjoy with your mates!

ALMOND + CHOCOLATE OVERNIGHT OATS

TYPE: Gluten-free, and, Soy-free

YIELD: 1-2 Servings

PREPARATION TIME: 5-10 Minutes

FRIDGE TIME: 7-8 Hours

INGREDIENTS ON THE GO

- 1/2 cup oats (you can opt for gluten-free too)
- 1/2 cup milk
- 2 Tbsp almond butter
- 1 Tbsp flaxseeds
- 1 Tbsp chopped dark chocolate

DIRECTIONS TO BE FOLLOWED

- Mix all ingredients all-together in an air-tight container OR mason jar and leave it in the fridge overnight.
- The next morning, follow with the toppings (like chocolate chips, almonds, blueberries, or anything you like).
- Enjoy every bite!

SWEET POTATOES WRAPS WITH TOFU

TYPE: Nut-free, and, Refined sugar-free

YIELD: 4 wraps approximately

TIME-TAKEN: 20-25 minutes

INGREDIENTS ON THE GO FOR SWEET POTATOES

- 2/3 sweet potatoes; properly peeled, and cut-off into cubes
- 1/4th cup peas
- 1 Tbsp coconut oil
- 1/2 Tbsp cumin seeds
- 1/2 Tbsp coriander
- 1/2 Tbsp turmeric powder
- Salt and Pepper as per your taste

INGREDIENTS ON THE GO FOR TOFU SCRAMBLE

- 1 packet tofu
- 1 small onion
- 1 Tbsp turmeric
- 1 Tbsp nutritional yeast
- 1 Tbsp garlic powder

- 1 Tbsp coconut oil
- Salt and Pepper as per your taste

INGREDIENTS ON THE GO for WRAP

- Whole wheat wraps
- Sliced Red/yellow bell pepper
- Sliced avocado

DIRECTIONS TO BE FOLLOWED

- For the sweet potatoes steam them in medium temperature for 10-15 minutes, until it is easily poked with a fork. Drain it when ready.
- For tofu, heat the coconut oil over medium heat; add the onions and sauce till being soft. To prevent burning, add splashes of water only if needed. Whilst the onions cook, gently squeeze water from the tofu and break it up into the frying pan. Add yeast, turmeric, garlic powder, pepper, and, salt. Cook for 5-10 minutes until poked easily. Transfer to a bowl.
- Back to the sweet potatoes; melt the coconut oil in a pan and add the drained potatoes. Mash the potatoes before adding spices. Mix it well and transfer to a plate.
- Put-in the potato filling and tofu to the wrap; you can do the topping with bell peppers or avocado.
- Enjoy every bite!

CLASSIC FRENCH TOASTING

TYPE: Sugar Filling

YIELD: 2-4 Slices

TIME-TAKEN: 10-15 minutes

INGREDIENTS ON THE GO

- 3/4 eggs
- 3/4th heavy cream
- 1/4th Tbsp vanilla extract
- 1/4th Tbsp cinnamon powder
- 6/7 slices of sour dough bread (neatly cut into 1/2 inch slices)
- Butter for frying
- 1 sliced banana
- 2 Tbsp brown sugar

DIRECTIONS TO BE FOLLOWED

- In bowl whist together eggs, cinnamon powder, vanilla extract, and heavy cream.
- Dip both sides of each bread slice into the egg mixture.
- Meanwhile, in a non-stick frying pan, melt 1 tbsp of butter.
- Fry the bread slices until golden brown (both sides).
- For making caramelized bananas, add on banana, brown sugar & butter to the pan.

- Once the sugar is caramelized, coat the bananas well enough.
- You can also do the toppings (lie caramelized bananas, raspberries, or maple syrup).
- Enjoy your Breakfast!

CHOCOLATE CHIA PUDDING

TYPE: Raw; Soy-free; Refined sugar-free; Nut-free; Oil-free, and, Gluten-free

YIELD: 2-3 cups

TIME-TAKEN: 5-10 minutes (2 hours for refrigerating chia seeds to gel)

INGREDIENTS ON THE GO (THE PUDDING)

- 3 Tbsp chia seeds
- 1 cup soy milk or coconut milk
- 5 chopped dates
- 1 Tbsp cocoa powder
- 1 Tbsp vanilla extract
- 1/8th Tbsp cinnamon

TOPPINGS

- 1/2 seeded pomegranate medium size
- 1 sliced banana
- Chopped dates
- 1-2 Tbsp sunflower seeds
- 1-2 Tbsp pumpkin seeds

DIRECTIONS TO BE FOLLOWED

- Mix the pudding in a jar or bowl. Stir it for 5-10 minutes and stir again to prevent any clumping.
- Cover it with a lid and let it refrigerate overnight.

- Mix it well before serving. Don't forget to add toppings.
- Enjoy every bite!

RIGHT and LIGHT SALADS

EAT YOUR GREENS TO
FIT INTO YOUR JEANS

LENTIL AND POTATO SALAD

TYPE: Sugar-free; Nut-free; Gluten-free, and, Soy-free

YIELD: 3-4 cups

TIME-TAKEN: 30-35 minutes

INGREDIENTS ON THE GO

- 1 Tbsp vegetable oil
- 1 diced onion
- 1 cup green lentil (soaked overnight)
- 1 cup of water
- 1/2 Tbsp turmeric powder
- 3/4th Tbsp salt
- 1/2 Tbsp ground cinnamon
- 1 diced potato

DIRECTIONS TO BE FOLLOWED

- Add oil and onion and sauté until brown, approximately 5-10 minutes.
- Add remaining ingredients; cover the lid partially, and heat it to a simmer.
- Stir once until lentils are soft enough and potatoes are very well-cooked, approximately 15-20 minutes.
- Enjoy!

QUINOA AND CHICKPEA SALAD

TYPE: Sugar-free; and, Gluten-free

YIELD: 5-6 servings

TIME-TAKEN: 20-25 minutes

INGREDIENTS ON THE GO FOR SALAD

- 2 cups cooked quinoa
- 1 cup cooked chickpeas
- 1 red and 1 yellow bell peppers
- 1 seeded and chopped tomato
- 1/3rd chopped cucumber
- 1 spring onion
- 1/4 cup olives chopped and pitted
- 1/4th cup cranberries
- 1/2 cup chopped almonds

INGREDIENTS ON THE GO FOR DRESSING

- 2 juiced lemons
- 2 Tbsp olive oil
- 8 cloves
- T Tbsp vinegar
- 1 Tbsp soy sauce
- 1 Tbsp sesame seed paste
- Salt and pepper according to the taste

DIRECTIONS TO BE FOLLOWED

- Pre-heat the oven to 200/390 C. With a bit of olive oil heat garlic for about 15-20 minutes until golden.
- Meanwhile, add the cut veggies, chickpeas, cranberries, and cooked quinoa in a bowl.
- Mash the roasted garlic and add the rest of the ingredients in it. Stir to continue.
- Pour the dressing onto the salad and toss to continue.
- Do the topping with almonds.
- Enjoy!

SAUSAGE TACO SALAD BOWL

A Quick Takeaway: This fantastic bowl is filled-in with proteins

- Beans
- Sunflower seeds
- Cashews
- Tofu

TYPE: Refined sugar-free; Gluten-free, and, Oil-free

YIELD: 2 main servings or 4 side servings (only if served with grains)

TIME-TAKEN: 20-25 minutes

INGREDIENTS ON THE GO: PEPPING ONTO THE BOWL

- 1/2 head lettuce - thinly cut
- 1/2 cooked beans (of your choice)
- Sausages (as per the requirement)
- 5-6 cherry tomatoes
- 1/2 avocado - thinly sliced
- 1/2 cup salsa
- 1/4 cup sunflower seeds
- 1/4 cup cilantro – diced
- Jalapeños

INGREDIENTS ON THE GO: For Cashew Dressing

- 1/3 cup raw cashews - soaked for an hour
- 1 lime juice
- 2 tsp cajun spice
- 30 ml of water

DIRECTIONS TO BE FOLLOWED

- Divide all salad ingredients between two medium size bowls.
- Add on 'Cashew Ingredients' to blender or food processor, and, blend on high until smooth. You can add water to your desired consistency.
- To the salad with the dressing!
- Enjoy every bite!

Hold on:

- Certain Variations: Add-on any other veggies of your choice, something like bell peppers or corn if you are into the enjoyment of salad. Also, you can make it a complete meal by adding whole grains like quinoa or Brown rice.
- Storage: Salad dressing can be stored in the refrigerator in an air-tight container for up to 3 days maximum.

SALAD ROLLS WITH A CREAMY PEANUT SAUCE

TYPE: Gluten-free

YIELD: 4/5 Rolls

TIME-TAKEN: 20 minutes

INGREDIENTS ON THE GO: SALAD ROLLS

- 1 Packet of rice noodles; softened in boiling water
- 1/2 cup frozen beans; thawed in boiling water
- 5 sheets of rice paper rolls
- 2 bell peppers; de-seeded, and, chopped into thin strips
- 1 carrot; peeled, and, cut into thin slices
- 1 cup thinly sliced or shredded red cabbage
- 1 avocado; cut into strips
- 1/2 cucumber; de-seeded, and, cut into thin slices

INGREDIENTS ON THE GO: SAUCE

- 1/4 cup creamy peanut butter
- 1/2 lime juice
- 1/4 hoisin sauce
- 2 tbsp water

OPTIONAL TOPPINGS - FOR DECORATION

- Sesame seeds
- Fresh cilantro
- Crushed peanuts
- Lime wedges
- Chili sauce

DIRECTIONS TO BE FOLLOWED

- Add the rice noodles and beans into respective bowls; pour on some boiling water. Keep them aside to soften.
- In a large bowl, soak 1 rice sheet in warm water for about 10 seconds; or till it gets soften. Make sure you don't over soak, else it will break.
- Remove the rice sheet from the water, and, let the excess water drip it off.
- Transfer the rice sheet to a large plate.
- Do the toppings with the drained rice noodles, avocado, or your favorite veggies
- Wrap the salad roll like a burrito, then, cut in half using a knife. Set aside!

MAKING OF THE SAUCE

- Combine the peanut butter, hoisin sauce, and, lime juice in a small bowl.

- Whisk it! Add small splashes of water somewhere about 5 ml and continue till the time you have got enough consistency.
- Serve with the salad rolls and Enjoy!

HOLD ON:

- Variations: Add crispy tofu; sautéed mushrooms; or fresh greens
- Storage: It can be stored in the refrigerator in an air-tight container for up to 3 days maximum.

MARINATED SESAME MUSHROOMS

TYPE: Gluten-free; Soy-free; Nut-free; Refined sugar-free

YIELD: 3/4 Cups

TIME-TAKEN: 10-15 Minutes

INGREDIENTS ON THE GO

- 3 cups sliced mushrooms
- 1 Tbsp soy sauce
- 1 tbsp vinegar
- 1/2 tbsp onion powder
- 1 tbsp sesame oil
- 1 cup cilantro - chopped (optional)
- 1 tbsp sesame seeds (optional)
- 3 small radishes - sliced (optional)
- Salt as per your taste

DIRECTIONS TO BE FOLLOWED

- Add all ingredients mentioned-above to a bowl, and, mix it well until combined.
- Serve on a bed of cilantro; sprinkle with sesame seeds.
- Do the topping with sliced radishes
- Enjoy every bite!

PURPOSEFUL BEVERAGES

A SIP, IT'S A REFRESHING LIFT

MELON CUCUMBER SODA

TYPE: Gluten-free; Nut-free; and, Soy-free

YIELD: 4/5 servings (depends on the size of cup)

TIME-TAKEN: 10-15 minutes

INGREDIENTS ON THE GO

- 4 cups honeydew melon - cut into small cubes
- 1/4 cup lime juice (almost 2 limes)
- 1/2 tbsp grated ginger
- 2 cups crushed ice
- 1/4 thinly sliced cucumber
- 1.5 cups carbonated water
- Maple syrup to taste

GARNISHING - OPTIONAL

- 1 lime - slightly chopped
- 3 tbsp granulated sugar

DIRECTIONS TO BE FOLLOWED

- Add the melon, lime juice, and, ginger to a blender. Keep blending until smooth.
- Use the lime for running around the rims of your serving glasses.
- Pour the sugar on a plate and dip the edge of the glass in the sugar just to create a decorative rim.

- Divide the crushed ice between the glasses; do the topping with the cucumber slices.
- Pour over top two parts blended melon mixture to one part carbonated water.
- Add maple syrup to taste, and, Enjoy!

HOLD ON

- Variations: You can add 1 tbsp fresh mint leaves blended for some tangy twist.
- Storage: You can store it in the refrigerator for up to 1 day only.

PINK LEMONADE

TYPE: Gluten-free; Soy-free; and, Nut-free

YIELD: 4/5 Servings (As per the size of the cup)

TIME-TAKEN: 15-20 Minutes

INGREDIENTS ON THE GO

- 2 Cups fresh or frozen raspberries
- Maple syrup as per the taste
- 4 lemons - juiced
- 4 cups cold water
- Ice cubes

GARNISHING - OPTIONAL

- Mint leaves
- Fresh raspberries
- Lemon slices

DIRECTIONS TO BE FOLLOWED

- Add on some raspberries and maple syrup to a pan on medium version and cook for 3-4 minutes. Prefer keeping the mixture at a simmer and as soon as the raspberries start to soften, use a wooden spatula gently for mashing them.
- Put on a sieve over a pitcher to strain the raspberry mixture; use the back of a spoon to press out as

much liquid from the mixture into the bowl. Let it cool-off.

- When cooled, stir in the lemon juice, cold water, also, ice. Stir it!
- Now, garnish with mint, raspberries, and lemon only if you desire.
- Enjoy!

HOLD ON

- Only if the drink is via too tart from the lemons, add maple as per your taste.
- Pink lemonade can be stored in a tight mason jar for up to 2-3 days.

BEETROOT LATTE

TYPE: Soy-free, Nut-free, and, Gluten-free

YIELD: 2-3 Servings

TIME-TAKEN: 10-15 Minutes

INGREDIENTS ON THE GO

- 2 cups unsweetened plant-based milk
- 1 steamed beetroot
- Dates - pits removed
- 1 tsp vanilla extract
- 1 stick of cinnamon

OPTIONAL INGREDIENTS

- 1 tbsp maple syrup
- 1 shot of espresso

DIRECTIONS TO BE FOLLOWED

- Combine all the above-mentioned ingredients in a blender; Keep them creamy and smooth.
- Pour this mixture in a pan onto medium heat and add a cinnamon stick. Let the mixture heat-up; keep a stir in-between just to prevent burning. Do the taste testing, and if you into more of a sweet tooth, add maple syrup accordingly.
- When it's cooked at a normal heat for about 3 minutes, remove the cinnamon stick.

- Pour a shot of espresso (optional) to a mug; pour onto your beetroot-infused milk.
- Stir it up and Enjoy!

BEING SPICY APPLE CIDER

TYPE: Soy-free; Nut-free; and, Gluten-free

YIELD: 6-7 Servings

TIME-TAKEN: 35-40 Minutes

INGREDIENTS ON THE GO

- 2 Litre apple juice or apple cider
- 1 orange - thinly sliced
- 4 cinnamon sticks
- 6 cracked cardamom pods
- 1/2 cup fresh cranberries
- 3 whole cloves
- 1 small piece ginger - thinly sliced

DIRECTIONS TO BE FOLLOWED

- Place all ingredients in a large bowl and boil over high heat.
- Reduce heat to a simmer; cover it partially and let infuse for approximately 30 minutes.
- Serve warm and Enjoy!

TARTING OVER APPLE TEA

TYPE: Gluten-free; Nut-free; Soy-free; Refined-sugar; and, Oil-free

YIELD: 4-5 Cups

TIME-TAKEN: 10-15 minutes

INGREDIENTS ON THE GO

- 3 tbsp dried rose petals
- 1 apple - thinly sliced
- 1 tbsp apple cider vinegar (ACV)
- 4 cups of water

DIRECTIONS TO BE FOLLOWED

- Add rose petals and apple to a pot and pour 4 cups of boiling water.
- Allow simmering for 10 minutes.
- Add the ACV at the end.
- Sweeten it a bit (only if desired)
- Enjoy!

COCONUT LATTE

TYPE: Nut-free; Gluten-free; Oil-free; and, Refined sugar-free

YIELD: 2/3 Servings

TIME-TAKEN: 5-10 Minutes

INGREDIENTS ON THE GO

- 1.5 cups of coconut milk
- 1/2 cup unsweetened plant-milk (you can also use soy)
- Dates
- 1 tsp matcha powder

DIRECTIONS TO BE FOLLOWED

- Blend all the mentioned ingredients in a blender until smooth.
- Transfer the mixture to a bowl on high heat and keep stirring just to avoid burning. When the liquid is hot (NOT BOILING), remove from heat and pour into your favorite mugs.
- Add a few drops of coconut milk or vanilla extract for a latte design (only if desired)
- Enjoy!

MUNCHING SNACKS

KUDOS! I AM YOURS!

BAKED ZUCCHINI CHIPS

TYPE: Low carb; and, Refined sugar-free

YIELD: 4/5 Servings

TIME-TAKEN: 3 Hours

INGREDIENTS ON THE GO

- 2 medium sized zucchini
- 1/2 tsp salt
- 1 tbsp oil

DIRECTIONS TO BE FOLLOWED

- Slice zucchini into thin rounds with a slicer.
- Place zucchini slices between paper towels to get rid of excessive moisture. Allow sitting in the refrigerator for 2 hours. NOTE: The drier the better!
- Combine the zucchini slices, salt, and, oil in a bowl. Toss to coat.
- Lay zucchini slices onto a parchment paper or silicone baking mat on top of a baking pan.
- Bake at 225 degrees F for almost 2-3 hours or until zucchini slices are on a road of their crisp.
- Serve with the spicy sauce and Enjoy!

COOKIES WITH CORNFLAKES

TYPE: Nut-free; and, Oil-free

YIELD: Servings as per the quantity taken

TIME-TAKEN: 40-50 Minutes

INGREDIENTS ON THE GO

- 1/4 teaspoon baking soda
- 3/4 cups flour
- 1/4 cup brown sugar
- 1/4 cup butter
- 1 teaspoon vanilla extract
- 2 tablespoon castor sugar
- 1/4 chocolate chips
- 1 egg
- 3/4 cups cornflakes

DIRECTIONS TO BE FOLLOWED

- Add baking soda and flour in a bowl.
- Separately, beat sugar and butter using an electric mixer until creamy and pale.
- Add-on 1 egg and beat until combined.
- Add the vanilla extract and mix.
- Crush cornflakes using your hands and mix in the dough well enough.

- Refrigerate the dough in the refrigerator for 25-30 minutes to chill.
- Till the time, the dough is in the refrigerator; pre-heat the oven at 180C.
- Scoop balls of dough using an ice-cream scoop onto your prepared trays.
- Flatten the dough balls carefully using your hands and do the topping with chocolate chips.
- Bake at 180C for nearly 15-20 minutes or till the time the edges become golden brown.

OPTIONAL TOPPINGS

- Cherries
- Gems
- Any Berries - Strawberries, Blackberries, or Raspberries

TRUFFLING WITH CHOCOLATE

TYPE: For Sweet Tooth Cravings

YIELD: Servings as per the quantity taken

TIME-TAKEN: 30-40 Minutes

INGREDIENTS ON THE GO

- 2 cups dark cooking chocolate
- 1 cup fresh cream

DIRECTIONS TO BE FOLLOWED

- Chop the dark chocolate finely and place it in a mixing bowl.
- In a non-stick pan, heat the fresh cream until warm. Make sure you don't burn it.
- Pour thé warm cream over the chopped chocolate; mix it well enough until the chocolate melts.
- Pour the fresh cream and chocolate mixture in a dish and let it rest in the refrigerator until it sets completely. The time-taken can be up to 30 minutes.
- Once the mixture sets completely, take it out of the refrigerator. Use a small ice-cream scoop or a spoon and roll them of equal sizes carefully.
- Roll the truffle balls into toppings.
- Refrigerate it for at-least 10-15 minutes before serving.

- Enjoy every bite!

OPTIONAL TOPPINGS

- Hershey syrup
- Cocoa powder
- Cashew nuts
- Pistachios
- Dried rose petals
- Coconut flakes

BANANA BREAD

TYPE: Gluten-free
YIELD: Servings as per the quantity taken
TIME-TAKEN: 30-40 Minutes

INGREDIENTS ON THE GO

- 1 cup gluten-free oats
- 1 cup tapioca flour
- 1 teaspoon baking powder
- 1/2 teaspoon baking soda
- 1 teaspoon cinnamon powder
- 1/2 teaspoon ginger powder
- 1/2 cup butter
- 2/3 eggs
- 1/4 cup castor sugar
- 3 large bananas - baked in the oven at 200C for about 10 minutes
- 1/2 pecans - crushed

DIRECTIONS TO BE FOLLOWED

- Pre-heat the oven to 180C. Line a loaf pan with parchment paper carefully.
- Whisk oats, flour, baking soda, baking powder, ginger, and, cinnamon in a bowl.
- Separately, beat sugar and butter.

- Add eggs and beat well enough.
- Mix the bananas and use a fork to make sure they are well-incorporated.
- Combine dry ingredients with the wet ingredients (don't over mix).
- Fold in the pecans.
- Transfer the batter into the loaf pan and bake at 180C for about 30-40 minutes.
- Once it cools down, do the topping with cream frosting.
- Enjoy!

VANILLA CHIA SEED PUDDING

TYPE: Gluten-free; Oil-free; Nut-free; and, Refined sugar-free

YIELD: 2/3 Servings

TIME-TAKEN: 20-25 Minutes

INGREDIENTS ON THE GO for CHIA PUDDING

- 1 cup coconut/soy/almond milk
- 3 tbsp chia seeds
- 1/4 teaspoon vanilla extract
- 1/8 teaspoon cinnamon

OPTIONAL INGREDIENTS

- 1/2 cup granola
- Strawberries; peach; blueberries
- 1 tbsp maple syrup
- 1/2 cup soy yogurt

DIRECTIONS TO BE FOLLOWED

- Gently whisk vanilla, milk, and chia seeds; let it wait for at least 10 minutes before giving it another stir. Then, cover and refrigerate for 2 hours or overnight for allowing the chia seeds to gel.
- Before serving, give one more stir with yogurt, fruits, and granola.

- Enjoy every bite!

NOTE: You can store in the refrigerator for up to 3 days.

WALNUT AND APPLE WARMLY CARAMELIZED

TYPE: Oil-free; and, Gluten-free

YIELD: 1/2 Cups

TIME-TAKEN: 20-25 Minutes

INGREDIENTS ON THE GO

- 1 apple - finely diced
- 1/2 cup wants - finely chopped
- 1/2 lemon - juice and zest
- 1 tsp sugar
- 1 tsp maple syrup
- 1/2 tsp cinnamon
- Pinch of salt

DIRECTIONS TO BE FOLLOWED

- Combine the apples, lemon juice, cinnamon, and salt into a bowl. Stir it!
- In a pan with medium-heat, toast the walnuts, sugar, and, maple syrup constantly for 4-5 minutes or until lightly caramelized.
- Mix the walnut mixture into the apple mixture.
- Let it sit for a while to soak up the flavors.
- Go ahead and Enjoy!

SIPPING SOUPS

DIVINE TASTE IN EVERY DROP

GREEN PEA SOUP

TYPE: Gluten-free

YIELD: 4-5 Servings

TIME-TAKEN: 25 Minutes

INGREDIENTS ON THE GO

- 2 tsp oil
- 2 cloves garlic - minced
- 1 small onion - diced
- 1 tsp thyme - dried
- 2 cups frozen peas
- 4 cups vegetable stock
- 1/2 cup cashews, drained salt & pepper - preferably soaked for 2 hours

DIRECTIONS TO BE FOLLOWED

- Take a large pan on medium-heat, cook garlic, onions, and oil; until onions are soft and golden for about 5 minutes. Add water as needed.
- Add the remaining ingredients, bring it to a boil, cover it partially with a lid, reduce the heat to low and let it sim for 15-20 minutes.
- Remove the pan from the heat and use a blender to blend the soup into a creamy touch.
- Do the toppings with croutons and Enjoy!

PEANUT BUTTER CURRY SOUP

TYPE: Gluten-free; and, Soy-free

YIELD: 4-5 Servings

TIME-TAKEN: 30 Minutes

INGREDIENTS ON THE GO

- 2 tsp oil
- 1 medium onion - diced
- 4 cloves garlic - minced
- 1 tbsp fresh ginger - minced
- 1 tbsp curry powder
- 2 tsp ground coriander
- 2 tsp paprika powder
- ⅛ tsp ground cayenne pepper
- 4 cups vegetable stock
- 2 sweet potatoes - peeled and cut into small cubes
- 1 yellow banana - cut into coins
- 1 carrot - peeled and chopped
- ½ cup peanut butter
- 1 can coconut milk

OPTIONAL TOPPINGS

- Fresh red chillies
- Fresh cilantro
- Coconut cream

- Toasted peanuts

DIRECTIONS TO BE FOLLOWED

- In a large pan onto medium-heat, add the oil, garlic, ginger, and onions. Cook for about 5 minutes. Add some water to prevent burning.
- Add the spices, stir it, and cook until fragrant for about 30 seconds.
- Add vegetable stock, banana, carrot, sweet potatoes, and, peanut butter. Bring it to a boil, reduce to a simmer, and cover it with a lid. Cook until the sweet potatoes are fork-tender for about 15 minutes.
- Add the coconut milk, and blend it.
- Heat completely and Enjoy!

NOTE: You can keep in an air-tight container in the refrigerator for up to 3 days.

LASAGNA SPINACH SOUP

TYPE: Nut-free; and, Refined sugar-free

YIELD: 4-5 Servings

TIME-TAKEN: 35 minutes

INGREDIENTS ON THE GO

- 2 tsp olive oil
- 1 yellow onion - diced
- 3 cloves garlic - minced
- 2 Tbsp tomato paste
- 1 tsp Italian seasoning
- 1 tsp dried oregano
- 1 tsp onion powder
- 1/2 tsp dried thyme leaves
- 1/4 tsp salt
- 1/4 tsp black pepper
- 1 package - veggie ground beef
- 2 cups mushrooms - diced
- 2 cans - diced tomatoes, with juice
- 2 tsp vinegar
- 8-10 uncooked lasagna noodles - broken into bite-sized pieces
- 2 cups fresh spinach

DIRECTIONS TO BE FOLLOWED

- Heat the oil in a large pan over medium-heat. Add the onion and sauté until slightly golden for about 5 minutes. Add a splash of water to deglaze the pan.
- Add tomato paste, garlic, spices; cook for 2-3 minutes. Afterwards, add the mushrooms and meat, cook, until the moisture from the mushrooms evaporates for about 5 minutes.
- Add the diced tomatoes and water from the cans, vinegar. Bring to a boil, then, add noodles. Cook for 10 minutes or till the time noodles is tender.
- In the end, stir in the spinach and remove the heat. Do the topping with fresh basil and Enjoy!

NOTE: You can store this up to 4 days in the refrigerator.

RAMEN-TO-GO SOUP

TYPE: Refined sugar-free; and, Nut-free

YIELD: 1-2 Servings

TIME-TAKEN: 10-15 Minutes

INGREDIENTS ON THE GO

- 1 block quick-cooking noodles
- 2 Tbsp miso paste
- 1/2 vegetable boullion cube
- 1/4 block tofu, cut into 1-inch cubes
- 3 medium mushrooms, - firmly sliced
- 1 green onion - thinly sliced
- 1 small handful spinach
- Sambal or other hot sauce to garnish - optional

DIRECTIONS TO BE FOLLOWED

- Layer the above-mentioned ingredients in a mason jar or other heat-proof container. Make sure noodles to go at the bottom, followed by the miso, vegetable cubes, tofu, green onion, and at last mushrooms and spinach.
- Keep in the refrigerator until ready to eat.
- When ready to eat, carefully pour boiling water into the container. Else, you can also transfer the contents into a bowl and then pour water.

- Add a cover and let it sit for 5-10 minutes or until the noodles are cooked as per your liking.
- Top on with spicy sauce
- Enjoy!

FOODIE MEALS

CONVERTING MOOD WITH FOOD

SPICY GARLIC TOFU

TYPE: Gluten-free; and, Nut-free

YIELD: 4-5 Servings

TIME-TAKEN: 25-30 Minutes

INGREDIENTS ON THE GO FOR TOFU

- 1 firm tofu - chopped into 1/2 inch cubes
- 1 tbsp vegetable oil
- 2 tbsp cornstarch
- 2 tsp black pepper
- 1/2 tsp salt

INGREDIENTS ON THE GO FOR SAUCE

- 5-6 cloves - minced
- 2 tbsp vegetable oil
- 1 red onion - diced
- 2-3 red chilies - thinly sliced
- 2 stalks green onion - thinly sliced
- 1/4 tbsp sesame seeds - toasted
- 2 tbsp maple syrup
- 1 tbsp chili paste
- 1 tbsp soy sauce
- 1 tbsp rice vinegar

DIRECTIONS TO BE FOLLOWED

- Drain any excess liquid out of the tofu before cutting into little cubes. The more liquid will be drained out, the quicker the tofu will cook making it more crispy.
- To a bowl, add the corn starch, vegetable oil, tofu cubes, pepper, and salt. Keep it gentle for tossing.
- Heat the pan and add the tofu, cook nearly about 10-15 minutes, or until crispy and golden. Make sure not to touch tofu via too much, else it will crumble. Toss a bit so that it cooks evenly on all sides.
- Meanwhile, make the sauce by mixing soy sauce, vinegar, maple syrup, and, chili sauce. Keep aside.
- When the tofu is crispy as per your liking, transfer it to another plate.
- Return to the same pan and heat-it up; add the vegetable oil. When hot, add chilis, garlic, and, green onion at once! Sauté for 5-10 minutes!
- Reduce the heat to medium-high; add the sauce being cooked for another 5 minutes or until the sauce becomes sticky.
- Add the tofu to the pan; stir it so that the tofu is fully coated.
- Garnish with sesame seeds.
- Serve and Enjoy!

COCONUT AND TOFU THAI RED CURRY

TYPE: Nut-free; Refined sugar-free; and, Gluten-free

YIELD: 4-5 Servings

TIME-TAKEN: 35 Minutes

INGREDIENTS ON THE GO: CURRY

- 1 tsp oil
- 4-5 shallots - peeled & minced
- 2 cloves - crushed
- 3 tbsp red curry paste
- 3 potatoes - chopped into chunks
- 2 red/yellow or carrots bell peppers - chopped
- 1 broccoli - chopped into bite sized bits
- Tofu strips
- 1 can of coconut milk
- 1 tbsp soy sauce
- 1 tsp hot sauce

OPTIONAL INGREDIENTS ON THE GO FOR GARNISH

- Basil or Cilantro or Parsley
- Roasted cashews
- Chilis flakes

DIRECTIONS TO BE FOLLOWED

- Sauté the shallots with oil in a pan on high-heat.
- Add 2 tbsp water s required to de-glaze the pan, avoid burning. Stir it until slightly browned. Later on, add cloves; stir it for the next 5 minutes and add water as required.
- Add the remaining ingredients and cook until fragrant and veggies are cooked as per your liking.
- Serve with brown rice or quinoa and Enjoy!

PAPRIKA PAELLA RICE

TYPE: Gluten-free; Soy-free; Nut-free

YIELD: 4-5 Servings

TIME-TAKEN: 60 Minutes

INGREDIENTS ON THE GO

- 1 tbsp olive oil
- 1 onion - chopped
- 2 cloves - minced
- 1 garlic
- 1 tsp salt
- 1 tsp black pepper
- 1 tsp smoked paprika
- 1 tsp dried thyme
- 1 tsp ground cumin
- 1 tsp dried oregano
- 2 tomatoes - diced
- 1 red/yellow bell pepper - thinly sliced
- 2 cups paella rice
- 4 cups boiling water
- 2/3 vegetable bouillon cubes
- 2 cups frozen green peas

OPTIONAL TOPPINGS FOR GARNISH

- 1 lemon
- 2 tbsp parsley - chopped

DIRECTIONS TO BE FOLLOWED

- Add oil to a pan onto medium-heat; once hot add cloves, garlic, onion, salt, and, pepper. Cook for 4-5 minutes, until the onions are brown.
- To the pan, add thyme, cumin, paprika, pepper, and oregano. Cook this whilst stirring for 30-60 seconds just to toast the spices.
- Add bell pepper and tomatoes, sauté for 5 minutes.
- Add the Paella rice and toast for 2-3 minutes. Stir occasionally.
- In a large jug, mix the boiling water and vegetable cubes.
- Add the liquid to the pan, avoid stirring.
- Bring the paella to a bit heat and let it sit for 5 minutes, then, turn the heat to a low sim heat and let it cook uncovered for at-least 20-30 minutes until tender.
- When the liquid has been absorbed by the rice, test them by eating a bit. If it's tender, they are ready. Else, you can continue to cook further if you want a bit more tenderness.
- Once properly cooked, add peas and bell pepper to the rice and stir it gently.
- Remove the pan from the heat; cover it with a lid for a few minutes; let the Paella rest for another 10 minutes. Make sure you don't skip this step because this will certainly make a lot of difference in the texture and taste of the rice.

- Now, remove the lid, do the toppings with parsley.
- Serve with lemon and Enjoy!

NOTE: You can store the paella in an air-tight container for up to 4 days in the refrigerator.

GARLIC POTATO QUESADILLAS

TYPE: Gluten-free; Nut-free; and, Refined sugar-free

YIELD: 4-5 Servings

TIME-TAKEN: 20-25 Minutes

INGREDIENTS ON THE GO FOR QUESADILLAS

- 1 tsp vegetable oil
- 3/4 red/yellow bell peppers
- 2/3 red onions
- 1 tsp cumin
- 1 tsp dried oregano
- 1 tsp paprika powder
- 4/5 tortillas
- 3-4 mashed potatoes

INGREDIENTS ON THE GO for SALSA

- 1 garlic - finely chopped
- 2 large tomatoes - diced
- 2 red onions - chopped
- 2 tsp salt
- 2 tsp chili powder
- 1 lemon - juiced

INGREDIENTS ON THE GO FOR GUACAMOLE

- 2 avocados - mashed
- 1 lemon - juiced
- 2 red onions - chopped
- 2 tsp cumin powder

DIRECTIONS TO BE FOLLOWED

- In a pan, heat 1 tsp vegetable oil and add-on onions and bell peppers. Sauté until brown and tender, for about 10 minutes. Add a bit of water for nourishment alongside spices, stir to mix. Once the water evaporates, keep aside.
- Prepare guacamole and salsa by adding all ingredients to a bowl and mix them. Keep aside.
- For preparing quesadillas, spread mashed potatoes filling on half of a tortilla. Add bell pepper and onion filling on top; softly fold the tortilla in another half.
- Heat 1 tsp of vegetable oil on medium-high; place two quesadillas in the pan and press down gently. Place a lid to ensure the filling warms-up. Once the tortillas turn crispy and golden, flip them and cook the other side.
- Repeat the process for the rest of the quesadillas.
- Cut it firmly and serve with salsa and guacamole.

BEANS AND RICE SALAD IN MASON JAR

TYPE: Nut-free; Soy-free; and, Gluten-free

YIELD: 4-5 Servings (Also, depending on the size of a jar)

TIME-TAKEN: 35-40 Minutes

INGREDIENTS ON THE GO

- 2/3 cups white rice

INGREDIENTS ON THE GO FOR DRESSING

- 1/2 cup olive/vegetable oil
- 1/2 cup fish lime juice
- 2 cloves of garlic - crushed
- 1 tsp ground cumin
- 2 tsp paprika powder
- 1/2 tsp black pepper
- 1 tsp salt

INGREDIENTS ON THE GO FOR SALAD

- 2/3 cups cherry tomatoes
- 1 cup cilantro leaves
- 2 avocados - diced
- 2 cups canned corn

- 2 red/yellow bell peppers - diced
- 2 cucumbers - diced
- 2 carrots - diced
- 2 red onions - diced
- 1 cup Jalapeno slices

INGREDIENTS ON THE GO FOR SPICED BEANS

- 1 tbsp olive/vegetable oil
- 3/4 cups cooked black beans/lentils/chickpeas
- 2 tsp garlic powder
- 2 tsp chili powder
- 2 tsp paprika powder
- 2 tsp onion powder
- 2 tsp ground cumin
- 1 tsp salt
- 1 tsp black pepper
- 1 tsp vinegar

DIRECTIONS TO BE FOLLOWED

- Cook the rice and let it cool off.
- Prepare the dressing by mixing all ingredients in a bowl. Keep them aside.
- In a pan, add the oil, beans, and spices. Cook for at-least 5-10 minutes. Keep stirring until the beans are covered in proper spices and well-cooked.
- Remove from the heat and let it cool-off completely.

ASSEMBLING MASON JAR

- Add rice; beans; bell pepper; corn; avocados; red onion; tomatoes; cucumbers; carrots.
- Do the topping with jalapeño and cilantro
- Mix it well before enjoying it!

NOTE: You can store this in the refrigerator for up to 4 days.

TOMATOES LOVES CHICKPEA

TYPE: Nut-free; refined sugar-free; soy-free

YIELD: 4-5 Servings

TIME-TAKEN: 35-40 Minutes

INGREDIENTS ON THE GO

- 2 tbsp olive/vegetable oil
- 1 onion - chopped
- 1/2 cups chickpeas - soaked overnight
- 1 yellow/red bell pepper - diced
- 2 tsp tomato paste OR chopped tomatoes
- 2 tsp cumin
- 2 tsp cinnamon

DIRECTIONS TO BE FOLLOWED

- Add all ingredients (except tomatoes) and 2 cups of water in a pan.
- Let it boil for once and reduce it to simmer, thus, covering it partially whilst stirring occasionally.
- Let it be for 30 minutes. Do a test tasting. Only if cooked, add the tomato paste.
- Serve whilst hot and enjoy!

SWEET TOOTH

SO GODAMN MELTY

YOGURT COVERED BLUEBERRIES

TYPE: Nut-free; Refined sugar-free; and, Gluten-free

YIELD: 3-4 Servings

TIME-TAKEN: 35-40 Minutes

INGREDIENTS ON THE GO

- 1 cup blueberries
- 1 cup yogurt or soy

DIRECTIONS TO BE FOLLOWED

- Gently mix the blueberries and yogurt in a bowl.
- Drop the mixture one-by-one onto a plate or baking sheet.
- Place the plate or the tray in the freezer.
- In a single layer, the berries will be frozen enough to handle in 30-35 minutes.
- Remove the berries from the tray or a plate; store them in an air-tight container in the freezer.
- Eat right away and Enjoy every bite!

NOTE: You can keep in the freezer for up to 1 month.

MANGO GINGER BITE

TYPE: Oil-free; Nut-free; Soy-free; and, Gluten-free

YIELD: 4-5 Servings

TIME-TAKEN: 4 Hours

INGREDIENTS ON THE GO

- 1 mango
- 1 lime - juiced
- 1 cup granulated sugar
- 1 tsp ground ginger
- 1 cup of water

DIRECTIONS TO BE FOLLOWE

- Head start by making a simple syrup solution - place the water in a pan on medium heat. Pour the sugar in the water and let it dissolve. NOTE: As soon as the sugar is dissolved completely, you can remove it from the heat.
- Peel, de-seed and scoop the mango flesh. Add it to a blender, alongside with the lime and ginger juice.
- Carefully and slowly pour the sugar syrup into the blender whilst it is running.
- Once everything is mixed, pour it to an air-container and let it freeze.
- Enjoy the icy taste!

SESAME TOUCH NUTTY

TYPE: Gluten-free

YIELD: 2/3 Cups

TIME-TAKEN: 20 Minutes approximately

INGREDIENTS ON THE GO

- 2 cups nuts of your choice - you can go for almonds or cashews or walnuts
- 2 tbsp maple syrup
- 1 tbsp coconut oil
- 1 tsp salt
- A pinch of cayenne pepper
- 2/3 tbsp sesame seeds

DIRECTIONS TO BE FOLLOWED

- Pre-heat oven to 180C
- Mix maple syrup, salt, coconut oil, and cayenne all-together in a bowl.
- Add in the nuts of your choice and toss to combine. Place on a baking sheet dedicatedly covered with a baking sheet; roast it for 5-10 minutes.
- Remove from the oven; add the sesame seeds; too to coat, and, roast for another 10 minutes, until fragrant. Make sure you don't over-cook them.

NOTE: You can store in an air-tight container for up to 2 weeks. Storage in a freezer can be up to 1 month.

SUGAR-FREE BROWNIE CHUNKS

TYPE: Oil-free; Gluten-free; and, Refined sugar-free

YIELD: 10 brownies approximately

TIME-TAKEN: 30 minutes

INGREDIENTS ON THE GO FOR BROWNIE CHUNKS

- 1 tbsp flax seeds
- 50 ml of water
- 10 dates - pitted
- 33 g cocoa powder
- 2 cups roasted hazelnuts
- 2 cup of soy milk
- 2 tsp vanilla extract
- 2 cups nut butter
- Coffee granules
- 2 tsp salt
- 2 cups chocolate chips or dark chocolate

DIRECTIONS TO BE FOLLOWED

- Foremost, pre-heat the oven to 180 C.
- In a bowl, combine the flaxseeds and water; let it sit for 5-10 minutes to gel.

- Till then, in a blender, add the hazelnuts and blend until you achieve a consistency like flour. Add to another bowl.
- Add the dates and blend until they turn into a soft ball.
- Transfer the mashed dates to the bowl and add the flaxseed gel; mix them until combined.
- Fill-in the batter in a mini-muffin container/tin. Bake for another 15-20 minutes until the top is firm enough. Let it cool-off before removing from the muffin tin.
- You can do topping with nuts or gems. Enjoy!

NOTE: You can store in the refrigerator for up to 3-4 days. If frozen, then for 1 month!

STRAWBERRY AND PECAN GRANOLA

TYPE: Gluten-free

YIELD: 10 servings approximately

TIME-TAKEN: 50 minutes

INGREDIENTS ON THE GO

- 5 cups oats
- 1 cup pecans - quartered
- 2 cups brown sugar
- 2 cups sunflower seeds
- 1 cup coconut flakes
- 1 cup pumpkin seeds
- 1 cup olive/vegetable oil
- 1/2 cup maple syrup (as per your taste)
- 1 tsp salt
- 2 cups strawberries
- 1 cup chia seeds

DIRECTIONS TO BE FOLLOWED

- Pre-heat oven to 180 C.
- Add all 'dry' ingredients to a bowl. Mix them until combined.
- Separately, mix together vegetable/olive oil, maple syrup, and, salt. Add them to the mixture of dry ingredients and stir to incorporate.

- Distribute in a casserole dish, perfectly lined with baking paper; place in the oven.
- In-between, remove from oven and stir every 10-15 minutes just to avoid burning. Once they are golden brown remove from the oven allow to cool for about 40-45 minutes.
- Once cooled, you can add chia seeds or nuts or any dried fruits. Stir to combine.
- Enjoy every bite!

Hey! Wait!

Our romance onto these recipes are not yet over and never will be. You keep sharing your love of recipes and let me find some more delicacies to impress your date.

Keep the wait ON. Until then, I will enjoy more book dates that are filled-in with some finger-licking ingredients of home cuisines.

Keep the hunger pangs booked!